Chakras, Colours and Drew the Dragon!

A child's second Spiritual book

By Eileen McCourt

Chakras, Crystals, Colours and Drew the Dragon!
A child's second Spiritual book

By Eileen McCourt

This book was first published in Great Britain in paperback during July 2018.

The moral right of Eileen McCourt is to be identified as the author of this work and has been asserted by her in accordance with the Copyright, Designs and Patents Act of 1988.

All rights are reserved and no part of this book may be produced or utilized in any format, or by any means, electronic or mechanical, including photocopying, recording or by any information storage or retrieval system, without prior permission in writing from the publishers – Coast & Country/Ads2life. ads2life@btinternet.com

All rights reserved.

ISBN-13: 978-1717879554

Copyright © July 2018 Eileen McCourt

Contents

Page

About the Author i

Acknowledgements vi

To parents and guardians vii

To all my young readers xi

PART ONE: CHAKRAS

Your 2 bodies 1

Your physical body and your 5 physical senses 5

Your Spiritual body and your 7 Chakras.......... 7

Cleansing your Chakras 17

Balancing your Chakras 23

Are your Chakras out of balance? 26

Meditating on your Chakras 42

PART TWO: CRYSTALS

Understanding crystals 52

Crystal colours and your Chakras 59

Page

Cleansing your Chakras with crystals 61

Energy of colours 70

The 7 colours of the Rainbow 85

Having a rainbow shower 92

ABOUT THE AUTHOR

Eileen McCourt is a retired school teacher of English and History with a Master's degree in History from University College Dublin.

She is also a Reiki Grand Master teacher and practitioner, having qualified in Ireland, England and Spain, and has introduced many of the newer modalities of Reiki healing energy into Ireland for the first time, from Spain and England. Eileen has qualified in England through the Lynda Bourne School of Enlightenment, and in Spain through the Spanish Federation of Reiki with Alessandra Rossin, Bienstar, Santa Eulalia, Ibiza.

Regular workshops and healing sessions are held in Elysium Wellness, Newry, County Down; New Moon Holistics N.I. Carrickfergus, County Antrim; Angel Times Limerick; Holistic Harmony Omagh, County Tyrone; Spirit 3 Ballinasloe, County Galway; Sacred Space Newbridge, County Kildare and Celtic School of Sound Healing, Swords, County Dublin, where Eileen teaches all of the following to both practitioner and teacher levels:

- Tibetan Usui Reiki levels 1, 2, 3 (Inner Master) 4 (teacher) and Grand Master

- Tera-Mai Reiki Seichem

- Okuna Reiki (Atlantean and Lemurian)

- Reiki Karuna (Indian)

- Rahanni Celestial Healing

- Fire Spirit Reiki (Christ Consciousness and Holy Spirit)

- Mother Mary Reiki

- Mary Magdalene Reiki

- Archangels Reiki

- Archangel Ascended Master Reiki

- Violet Flame Reiki

- Lemurian Crystal Reiki

- Golden Eagle Reiki (Native North American Indian)

- Golden Chalice Reiki

- Golden Rainbow Ray Reiki

- Goddesses of Light Reiki

- Unicorn Reiki

- Pegasus Reiki

- Elementals Reiki

- Dragon Reiki

- Dolphin Reiki

- Pyramid of Goddess Isis Reiki

- Magnified Healing of the God Most High of the Universe

- Psychic Surgery

This is Eileen's **16th** book. It is the sequel to '*Rainbows, Angels and Unicorns*' a child's first spiritual book.

Previous publications include:

- '*Living the Magic*', published in December 2014

- '*This Great Awakening*', September 2015

- '*Spirit Calling! Are You Listening?*', January 2016

- *'Working With Spirit: A World of Healing'*, January 2016

- *'Life's But A Game! Go With The Flow!'*, March 2016

- *'Rainbows, Angels and Unicorns!'*, April 2016

- *'........And That's The Gospel Truth!'*, September 2016

- *'The Almost Immaculate Deception! The Greatest Scam in History?'*, September 2016

- *'Are Ye Not Gods?' The true inner meanings of Jesus' teachings and messages'*, March 2017

- *'Jesus Lost and Found'*, July 2017

- *'Behind Every Great Man...... Mary Magdalene Twin Flame of Jesus'*, July 2017

- *'Out of the Mind and into the Heart: Our Spiritual Journey with Mary Magdalene'*, August 2017

- *'Divinely Designed: The Oneness of the*

iv

Totality of ALL THAT IS', January 2018

- 'Resurrection or Resuscitation? What really happened in That Tomb?', May 2018

- 'Music of the Spheres: Connecting to the Great Universal Consciousness and to ALL THAT IS through the music of Irish composer /pianist Pat McCourt', June 2018

Eileen has also recorded 6 guided meditation cds with her brother, pianist Pat McCourt:

- 'Celestial Healing'

- 'Celestial Presence'

- 'Cleansing, energising and balancing the Chakras'

- 'Ethereal Spirit'

- 'Open the Door to Archangel Michael'

- 'Healing with Archangel Raphael'

All publications are available from Amazon online and all publications and cds are in Angel and Holistic centres around the country, as specified on website, www.celestialhealing8.co.uk

ACKNOWLEDGEMENTS

As always, my heart-felt thanks to my publishers, Don Hale OBE and Dr. Steve Green for their patience, advice and input. Dr. Steve Green has certainly excelled himself in this publication with his delightful illustrations! Thank you, Steve! You truly are amazing!

And my sincere thanks, yet again, to all who have been constantly supporting and encouraging me in my work. You all know who you are!

Sincere and heart-felt appreciation to all of you who are buying my books and cds and for your kind comments.

Thank you to all who attend my workshops and courses, and to all who have taken the time to write reviews for me, both in my books and on Amazon. You are greatly appreciated!

Finally, as always, I give thanks for all the wonderful blessings that are constantly being bestowed upon us in this wonderful, loving, abundant Universe.

Namaste!

7th July, 2018

TO PARENTS AND GUARDIANS

We are going through a great Spiritual awakening at this point in time. A great upward shift in energy is taking place on our Planet Earth, raising our Spiritual Consciousness, taking our Soul Awareness to a higher vibrational energy level than ever before in the history of mankind.

We are on the cusp of something great, a huge upward movement that has less to do with religion and more to do with Spirituality.

Spirituality transcends religion. Spirituality is all about connecting with what lies beyond our five physical human senses. It is a deep desire, a longing, a searching to find and appreciate more than we can see and hear in what we consider to be our surrounding natural reality.

Our children are much more tuned into all things Spiritual than we adults are. But our education systems do not further or encourage their inherent knowing that there is a vast Spiritual reservoir all around us into which we can constantly tap, unseen worlds beyond our limited human vision, hands reaching out to us from higher energy vibrational levels, all helping to raise our Spiritual Consciousness and bring us further along the path of our own Spiritual Ascension.

Our children need to be taught the truth about all matters Spiritual. Only when they know the truth can their beautiful souls soar and fly freely, as they are meant to do. Only when they know the truth can their beautiful souls sing their own glorious, rapturous song, in the harmony of the One great cosmic orchestra.

We are empowering our young people when we give them knowledge and the truth. In this book, they will learn about their Chakra system, the importance of colour in our lives and how we can all use crystals and colour to heal and to enhance our quality of life.

There is no better gift you can give a young person than the gift of empowerment. And the purpose of this book is to do just that. To provide simple tools to help children gain knowledge, and through knowledge, empowerment. It is a follow-on from the previous book '*Rainbows, Angels and Unicorns*', in that it is a basic introduction to Chakras and how children can care for and nurture their Spiritual energy body as well as their physical body.

When you read this book with your child on a daily basis, you will indeed be empowering them to live life with their own power, strength, energy, understanding and balance.

Together, let us equip our young children with the knowledge they need in order to advance along their Spiritual path and to make this world a better place for everyone! Let us help them to express themselves with love, light, joy and caring. Children exude innocence, beauty, a peaceful Spirit, a delight in discovering everything around them, a love of Nature and a naturally creative character. Let us help them to find confidence and courage within themselves to live a truly joyful and positive life, radiating peace and love out to all whom they meet on their journey of life. May their Spiritual light shine out to all!

Finally, as a note of caution! The information contained in this book is not meant as a substitute for medical advice or treatment, either in the case of physical ill-health or mental ill-health. The information is merely a guide-line as to how your child can be more positive and confident in every day life, and is intended to work hand in hand with Western medicine, not instead of it. If you feel concerned about your child, then you should always contact your medical doctor for advice and follow that advice.

And a further note of caution! Please do not leave young children unsupervised around crystals! Crystals are very appealing, attractive and alluring to young children and many of them, especially the tumbled stones varieties can seem like candy or sweets and can often find their way into a child's mouth! So please, for safety, be sure to leave all crystals out of reach of young children!

I send you all Love and Light!

Namaste!

Eileen McCourt

TO ALL MY YOUNG READERS!

Hello again all you beautiful young people!

This is the second book written especially for you!

In the first book, '**Rainbows, Angels and Unicorns**', you met Maggie and Mattie who helped you to understand exactly who you really are and why you are so special. You learned lots of things about yourself that you are not taught in school. You learned all about energy, how we are all forms of energy, changing all the time, and you learned that we each have two bodies. You learned about your Aura, and you learned about all the little Nature Spirits who look after the flowers and trees.

And you learned about God and Angels. You learned that God is the Great White Light, and that nothing or no-one can exist outside of that Great White Light. We are all included in that Great God Energy and we are all One. Remember all that?

Well, it is now time for you to learn some more!

It is time for you to learn about your Chakras, and more about Crystals and colours, and of course, the colours of the Rainbow!

All very exciting! And all great fun! And definitely not like school!

And Maggie and Mattie are here once again to help you understand, this time, about your Chakras, and to tell you more about Crystals and those beautiful Rainbows you see in the sky! and with them is their friend Drew the dragon! Drew wants to be your friend too!

So let us join Maggie Mattie and Drew through the pages of this book to find out what they have learned since they were last with you and what they can tell us. And just like the last book, you can colour in all the pictures, and make this book your own very special book. A very special book for a very special person.

Yes, the world is so much better for having you in it! You are the future of our world, and you will indeed restore our world to balance and health, through spreading your beautiful shining Spiritual light wherever you go, and bringing peace, joy and love to all!

Thank you for being you!

But before we start, I invite you to meet Mattie and Maggie and their friend Drew!

Chakras, Crystals, Colours and Drew the Dragon!

PART ONE: CHAKRAS
YOUR 2 BODIES

Do you remember learning in '**Rainbows, Angels and Unicorns**' that you actually have two bodies?

And do you remember what those two bodies are called? And why you have two bodies?

One is called your physical body, and the other is called your Spiritual body. Your physical body is the body everyone sees and which you see in the mirror. This is the body that makes you able to run and jump and do all the other things you do every day.

Your physical body has a heart, a brain and all the other organs that all work together to keep you alive.

But this physical body of yours is only temporary. That means it will not go on living forever. Some day you will find that it is no longer of any use to you, and you will get rid of it in just the same way as you get rid of your old worn-out clothes.

But your Spiritual body, sometimes called your Energy body, or your Soul is not like your physical body. Your Spiritual body is immortal, which means it will go on living forever.

While your physical body is visible to you and everyone else, your Spiritual body on the other hand, cannot be seen by you or anyone else. It is Spiritual, and Spiritual things cannot be picked up through our five physical senses.

And your physical body and your Spiritual body work together to make up the whole you. They work together to make sure that you are living a happy, contented life, full of fun and laughter, enjoying what you are doing.

While your physical body has 5 senses, your Spiritual body, on the other hand has **7 Chakras**. Let us look at all of these more

Chakras, Crystals, Colours and Drew the Dragon!

closely!

Eileen McCourt

YOUR PHYSICAL BODY AND YOUR 5 PHYSICAL SENSES

Your physical body has 5 senses, through which you are able to connect with the physical world all around you and through which you can experience all that this wonderful world of ours has to offer.

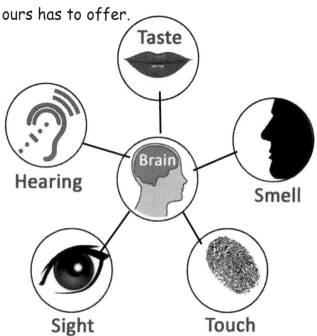

You see, you hear, you feel, you smell and you taste. Without these 5 physical senses, you would just be like a robot or a computer, unable to interact with other people or other forms of life around you.

And you know what? These 5 physical senses all work together. So if one of them is not functioning properly, all the others make up for that or compensate for it. For example, if someone's eyesight is not as good it should be, then that person's sense of hearing or sense of feeling will be strengthened to work harder!

YOUR SPIRITUAL BODY AND YOUR 7 CHAKRAS

In just the same way as your physical body has **5** physical senses, which connect you to the world all around you, so too, your Spiritual body has also got senses, or energy centres. These are called your **Chakras**, (pronounced **shack-rahs**) and you have **7** of them, all a different colour and all fulfilling a different function for your Spiritual body.

Your **7 Chakras** all work together to connect your physical body to your Spiritual body and to the Great God Energy. The word *'Chakra'* is a very ancient word, meaning *'wheel of light'*. Your Chakras are spinning round all the time, just like great spinning discs or wheels of colour and light, all creating energy, which in turn feeds into your physical body.

They are all lined up in a straight line along

Chakras, Crystals, Colours and Drew the Dragon!

your spine, front and back, from the bottom of your spine to the very top of your head.

Each Chakra is connected to a different aspect of your Spiritual life and gives energy to that part of your life.

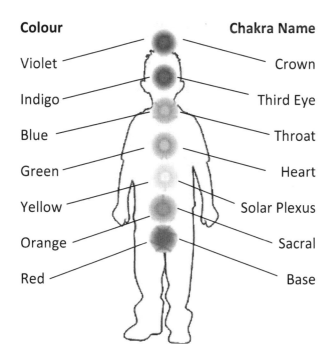

Colour	Chakra Name
Violet	Crown
Indigo	Third Eye
Blue	Throat
Green	Heart
Yellow	Solar Plexus
Orange	Sacral
Red	Base

Your **1st Chakra** is called your Base or your Root Chakra, because it is at the base of your spine, at the bottom of your backbone, and because it is all about your roots. That means it is connected to your thoughts of your survival in this lifetime, in particular your family, your thoughts of safety and security, your thoughts of all the material things you need in order to live, such as your food, your clothes, your house, money and all the other things you need in everyday living. This Chakra is **red** in colour.

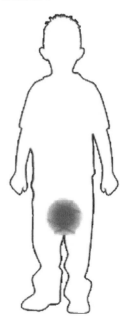

Chakras, Crystals, Colours and Drew the Dragon!

Your **2nd Chakra**, this one coloured **orange**, is just above your red Base Chakra, between the bottom of your backbone and your belly button. This **orange Chakra** is connected to your ability to create and think up great ideas, and to enjoy certain activities, such as your hobbies, painting, baking or playing sports. This Chakra is also about the relationship you have with yourself and with other people.

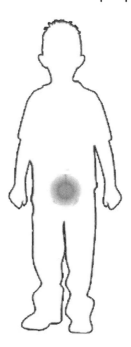

9

Your **3rd Chakra, coloured yellow**, is just right above your belly button. This Chakra is connected to your power, so we sometimes call it our *'power-house'*. This is where we get the power and the strength to do whatever we need to do, to make decisions, and to help us through difficult times. This **3rd Chakra** is your centre of feeling, where you often get that *'gut'* feeling about something or someone.

Chakras, Crystals, Colours and Drew the Dragon!

Your **4th Chakra** is your **Heart Chakra**, on your heart of course. This is the centre of love in your body, from where you send out love and light to everyone around you, and of course, where you feel love for yourself. It is a beautiful **green** colour with specks of **pink**.

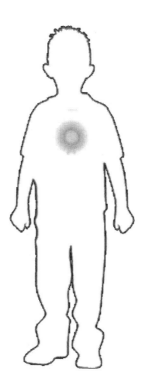

Your **5th Chakra** is your **Throat Chakra**, known as your **Communication Chakra**, because it is from here that you communicate with other people, expressing yourself clearly, telling them your thoughts and ideas, and speaking the truth. This Chakra is **light blue**, the colour of the sky.

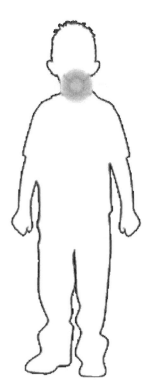

Chakras, Crystals, Colours and Drew the Dragon!

Your **6th Chakra** is at your **Third Eye**, your inner eye, right in the middle of your forehead. This is your centre of knowing and understanding, which helps you know when something is right or wrong. It is like a movie-house, where you see pictures of all sorts of things about your friends, your family, your life. These pictures come from God and the Angels, through your Third Eye, which is also called your **Intuition Eye**. That means you see things with this Third Eye which you do not see with your human eyes. And sometimes you just know things without anyone telling you. This **Third Eye Chakra** is coloured **indigo**, which is a shade of **dark blue**, like the colour of the ocean.

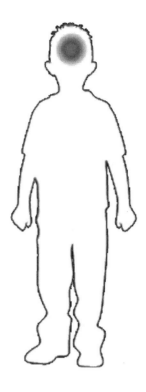

Finally, your **7th Chakra**, right on the top of your crown, called your **Crown Chakra**. This is the Chakra that connects you to the Great God Light, the Great God Energy. This is coloured **violet or deep purple**, sometimes with **gold** or **white** flecks running through it. This is where you receive the messages that God and the

Angels are sending you. This **Crown Chakra** is usually very obvious in a young baby. If you look at the crown of your baby sister's or baby brother's head, you will see a small circular shape. That is the **Crown Chakra**, easily visible before hair begins to grow over it.

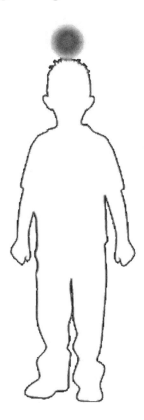

So now you know where your **7 Chakras** are on your body, and the purpose for each one.

You need to keep your Chakras healthy. That means you need to keep them clean, shining brightly and all spinning at the same speed, all in balance.

So now, let us see first of all how you can clean and clear your Chakras.

You can't go in the shower and wash them, or soak them in the bath! That's for your physical body only!

So how do you clean and clear your **Chakras**, your Spiritual energy centres?

Chakras, Crystals, Colours and Drew the Dragon!

CLEANSING YOUR CHAKRAS

Now that you know about your **7 Chakras**, it is time to learn how to clean and clear them!

Find a quiet comfortable place to sit or lie down. Close your eyes and breathe deeply. Imagine a great beautiful white light filling up the space around you. As you breathe in, feel your entire body being filled with this beautiful white light. As you breathe out, let the white light flow out of your body. Keep breathing the white light in and out.

Now, imagine your **red Chakra**. As the white light flows over it, see the white light itself turn to red, cleaning and clearing your **red Chakra**, making it sparkle and shine even more!

17

Next, see the white light move over your **orange Chakra,** and as it does so, the white light itself turns to orange, cleaning and clearing your **orange Chakra**, making it sparkle and shine even more!

Now, see the white light move over your **yellow Chakra**, and as it does so, the white light itself turns to yellow, cleaning and clearing your **yellow Chakra**, making it sparkle and shine even more!

Chakras, Crystals, Colours and Drew the Dragon!

The white light now moves over your **green and pink Heart Chakra**, and as it does so, the white light itself changes into green and pink, cleaning and clearing your **green and pink Heart Chakra**, making it sparkle and shine even more!

Next, see the white light move over your **pale blue Throat Chakra**, and as it does so, the white light itself changes into pale blue, cleaning and clearing your **pale blue Throat Chakra**, making it sparkle and shine even more!

Now see the white light move over your **indigo Third Eye Chakra**, and as it does so, the white light itself changes colour into indigo or dark blue, cleaning and clearing your **indigo Third Eye**, making it sparkle and shine even more!

Finally, see the white light move over your **violet or purple Crown Chakra**, and as it does so, the white light itself changes into violet or purple, cleaning and clearing your **violet Crown Chakra**, making it

sparkle and shine even more!

To end, breathe the white light in deeply once again, and feel it filling your entire body. Now, as you breathe out, feel all your worries, problems and fears, and anything that has been upsetting you or causing you concern or making you unhappy, feel all of that flowing out of your body with the white light. The white light is taking it all away back down to Mother Earth, where Mother Earth will deal with it. That is exactly what Mother Earth does!

How good you feel now! All your **7 Chakras** cleaned and sparkling!

WOW!

BALANCING YOUR CHAKRAS

For you to be healthy, you need to have your **7 Chakras** not only clear and clean, but also all balanced and spinning at the same speed.

Here is a simple exercise for you to help balance all your **7 Chakras.**

All you need is a quiet place to sit, and of course, your imagination!

To begin, find a quiet place to either sit or lie down. Breathe in deeply three times, letting yourself become very relaxed.

Now, close your eyes and see your Spiritual body in front of you, as if you are looking in a mirror.

Look at each of your Chakras in turn, starting with the red, then working upwards through the orange, the yellow, the green / pink, the pale blue, the indigo, and finally the violet or purple.

See each Chakra sparkling and glowing in your body.

Look carefully and see if they are all the same size. If not, then using your imagination, make them all the same size.

Are they all spinning at the same rate? If not, then again using your imagination, make them all spin at the same speed. Start with your red Chakra. Make it spin as best you can. Then make your orange Chakra spin at the same speed as your red Chakra. Now make your yellow Chakra spin like the orange and red Chakras.

And so on, work your way up to your violet or purple Crown Chakra, making them all spin at the same speed.

When you have them all the same size and all spinning at the same speed, then your Chakras are balanced.

Chakras, Crystals, Colours and Drew the Dragon!

Finally, breathe in deeply and see and feel the beautiful white light filling your whole body, and of course, making your **7 Chakras** all sparkle and glow!

7 beautiful, sparkling, glowing little **coloured jewels**, all sparkling and glowing and sending energy through your whole body!

How good is that!

Eileen McCourt

ARE YOUR CHAKRAS OUT OF BALANCE?

As you have just learned, for you to be happy and healthy and full of the joys of living, your **7 Chakras** all need to be spinning round at the same speed. And all shining brightly! Like **7** little sparkling, spinning, coloured jewels. Whirlpools of colour, little magical balls, reflecting your emotions and feelings!

But how do you know when this is not the case? How do you know when your **7** Chakras are not working properly? When they are blocked? When one of these little jewels is not sparkling brightly, or is not spinning like the others? When they are not all spinning at the same rate?

Well there are signs for you to look for, and these signs will let you know what is happening with your **Chakras**.

Chakras, Crystals, Colours and Drew the Dragon!

For example, you might not be feeling just as happy as you should be feeling, or as happy as you were a few days ago, or not as healthy as you should be feeling. Or you might be feeling hurt or angry with someone. Or scared. Or alone. Or guilty. Or maybe you are not feeling very enthusiastic about what you are doing, or maybe you are feeling bored and fed up. These feelings, which you feel in your physical body are all a sign that all is not as well as it should be in your **Chakras**.

Remember, you have already learned that your **7 Chakras** connect your physical body to your Spiritual body. And your **Chakras** are your energy centres in your Spiritual body. Remember all that? So when you get these feelings in your physical body, then you need to think about which of your **7 Chakras** is not in balance with all the other Chakras.

So let us now take a look at each Chakra in turn and try and work out which Chakra is not in

27

balance!

We will start with the **1st Chakra.** Remember, that's the **red Chakra** at the bottom of your tailbone, at the base of your spine.

You will know if it is this **red Chakra** that is not spinning properly or the same as all the others if you are feeling frightened of something or you cannot sleep at night, or if you are greedy and overeating or if you want

Chakras, Crystals, Colours and Drew the Dragon!

too many material possessions, or if you do not like living where you are living. Also if you have low self-esteem. This means that you do not see yourself as the great and wonderful person you really and truly are!

Now let us change this picture!

You will know that this **red Chakra** is spinning properly, the same as all the others, if you are feeling safe and secure, and you are happy being you, you are comfortable in your own skin, or you love where you are living. Also when you feel confident in everything that you do.

Let's move to your **2nd Chakra** now, the **orange Chakra**, just above your red Chakra, and below your belly button. You will know that it is this **orange Chakra** that is not spinning properly like all the

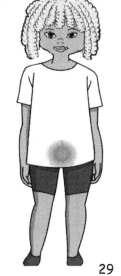

others if you are feeling bored or uninterested in what is going on around you, or if you feel no enthusiasm or excitement for anything as you go through your day. In other words, if you are just moping about the place, complaining all the time, with a glum face on you for everyone to see, and waiting for something or someone to wave a magic wand and make you happy again.

Now let us change this picture!

You will know this **orange Chakra** is working properly if you are feeling creative and enjoying life through doing what you love doing, for example, painting, playing sports, making things, or partying with your family or friends. In other words, when you are enjoying yourself and having a fun time!

Chakras, Crystals, Colours and Drew the Dragon!

Now for your **3rd Chakra**, your **yellow Chakra**, just above your belly button. How will you know if this **yellow Chakra** is not working properly? Well, a sure sign will be if you are feeling bad about yourself, or see yourself as not as good as someone else. In other words, if you have low self-esteem,  or you lack confidence in yourself. Also if you are angry with other people, bully them or you are being aggressive towards them and picking fights and arguments. Or if you are always blaming other people rather than seeing that you are the one to blame!

Now let us change this picture!

You will know that this **yellow Chakra** is working properly if you are being responsible and reliable, if you feel that you are very worthy and deserve only the best, if you are warm and generous towards others, if you are playful and full of fun, and full of confidence that you do your best at everything.

Next, what about your **4th Chakra**? Remember, this is your Heart Chakra, the **green Chakra** with little specks of pink, right in the middle of your chest. You will know this **green Chakra** is not working properly if you are feeling jealous of anyone, or feeling sorry for yourself, trying to please everyone too much, criticising others, or feeling impatient or intolerant of

others. Also if you don't want to join with your friends in having fun, or not showing them you care about them.

Now let us change this picture!

You will know this **green and pink Heart**

Chakras, Crystals, Colours and Drew the Dragon!

Chakra is working properly when you feel caring and loving towards other people, trying to help whenever you can, and when you love yourself. Loving yourself does not mean getting and asking for all the material goods you can get. Or thinking that you are better than anyone else! No! Remember, as you have just seen, this means that your red Chakra is not working properly! But we are talking about your **Heart Chakra** now, your **green and pink Chakra**. And about loving yourself. And how do you love yourself? By seeing yourself as the bright shining light you really are, and not just a physical body. And when you see yourself as that bright shining light, shining out to everyone you meet, you will not judge yourself or feel guilty or criticise yourself or feel bad about yourself, simply because you see yourself as the best, and because you see yourself as the best, you deserve only the best. That's how you love yourself! And you have to love yourself first before you can love anyone else!

And if you do not love yourself and who you are, then how can you expect anyone else to love you?

Now let's look at your **5th Chakra**, your **Throat Chakra**, the **pale blue Chakra** right on your throat. If this **blue Chakra** is not working properly, then you must be gossiping about someone or saying cruel things to someone, or hurting them by what you are saying to them, or saying about them to other people. Also if you have difficulty telling the truth about everything or trying to cover up what you have done by telling lies. Or if you are afraid to speak the truth, maybe because you think others will not like you for doing so. Or if someone tells you something in confidence, and you go and tell someone else! All of this shows that your **pale blue Throat Chakra** is not

Chakras, Crystals, Colours and Drew the Dragon!

working properly.

Now let us change this picture!

You will know that your **blue Throat Chakra** is working properly when you are telling the truth and owning up to what you have done, or when you are saying only good things about other people and not hurting them with unkind remarks. If you have nothing good to say about someone, then it is best if you say nothing at all about them! You will know your **pale blue Throat Chakra** is working properly also when you stand up for someone who has been wrongly accused of something they did not do, and you are not afraid to be the odd one out in doing this, or afraid of what others will think of you. It is no good keeping quiet and saying nothing if the truth is being kept hidden and you are afraid of speaking out and telling what you know to be the truth.

Next, your **6th Chakra,** your **Third Eye**, right in the middle of your forehead, a lovely **indigo** colour, like a light purple or deep blue. You will know this Chakra is not working properly when you cannot get your imagination to work, when you have difficulty creating things, when you are confused when making decisions, when you cannot remember things, when you are not trying to improve yourself, or when you cannot see the truth of what is going on around you, in other words, when you literally cannot see what is going on. That means you are not understanding things properly, perhaps you are just in denial and refusing to accept what is going on around you because you do not like it. Also when you have difficulty concentrating or paying attention. Or if you have a bad nightmare, that could be a sign that

36

Chakras, Crystals, Colours and Drew the Dragon!

your **indigo Third Eye Chakra** is not working properly.

Now let us change this picture!

You will know that your **Third Eye Chakra**, coloured **indigo**, is working properly when you are able to imagine all sorts of things, when you are able to make sensible and wise decisions, when you are able to see what lies beneath the surface. In other words, when you are able to see deeply into a person or situation. Also when you remember things well. God and the Angels put pictures into your Third Eye, pictures which you cannot see with your two physical eyes. Remember, your Third Eye is a Spiritual Eye and because it is a Spiritual Eye, you can see things through it that your two physical eyes cannot see. Your two physical eyes can only see things that are in existence around you, material things. But your **Third Eye**! That lets you see much deeper! That lets you see into many of the other forms of energy that are all around us, like the Fairy Worlds and the Angels. Do you remember learning in *'Rainbows, Angels and Unicorns'* how we are all energy, and surrounded by numerous other energy levels? Well, it is through your amazing **Third Eye Chakra** that you can see or sense these other energies.

Finally, let us look at your **7th Chakra,** your **Crown Chakra**, right at the top of your head, and coloured **purple or violet.** When this Chakra is not working or spinning properly, you are feeling confused about things and trying to over-think things. Sometimes you cannot get your head around all the information you are being given in school or in books, and that is a sign that your **Crown Chakra** is not as balanced as it could be.

Now let us change this picture!

Chakras, Crystals, Colours and Drew the Dragon!

When your **violet Crown Chakra** is working properly, you feel you are a bright shining light, and that is your Spiritual connection, you connecting with your Spiritual body. Your **Crown Chakra** is your direct link to God and all things Spiritual. Through your **Crown Chakra**, you feel you are always being looked after by God and the Angels, and you just know that you will never be alone or left on your own to cope with whatever comes your way in your life.

So you see, it is very easy for you to work out which of your **7 Chakras** might be out of balance! They all need to be shining brightly and spinning at the same speed.

Just picture in your mind **7 little coloured jewels**, all lined up in a straight line, up through your body, front and back. And you know the colour of each little sparkling jewel!

So, as a reminder, let's start at the top this time and work our way downwards!

Purple or violet

Indigo or a shade of dark blue or lavender

Blue

Green and pink

Yellow

Orange

Red

Imagine them all spinning together at the same speed, all clean and bright, in a beautiful sequence of colour, little sparkling jewels spinning all through your body!

And you already know how to get them all spinning together, sparkling and shining brightly. And you know you need to keep them clean and balanced! And you learned all about how to clean them in chapter 4 and how to balance them in chapter 5.

And when your **7 Chakras** are all clear and sparkling, and all in balance, spinning at the same speed, then your Spiritual body is very healthy indeed!

How wonderful is that!

WOW!

What an amazing feeling!

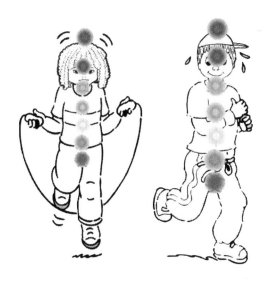

Eileen McCourt

MEDITATING ON YOUR CHAKRAS

Here is an amazing exercise you can do that will give you the most wonderful feeling!

This is what we call the **'I AM'** exercise! It will fill you full of that feel-good factor! You will feel confident, full of joy and love, happy and full of fun, loving your life and loving who you are, loving just being you!

So what do we have to do? How do we get ourselves to feel like this?

To begin, sit very still and quietly, away from all the noise. You can sit on a chair with your back straight, or you can sit in what is called the *lotus* or *yogi* position.

Now you are going to concentrate on each Chakra in turn, saying positive words to yourself.

Ready?

Breathe deeply, 3 times.

Think of your body as a beautiful rainbow, with all the **7 colours** of the rainbow sparkling through it.

First, concentrate on your **root Chakra**, that's the **red Chakra** at the base of your spine. Say these words to yourself or out loud and really mean them!

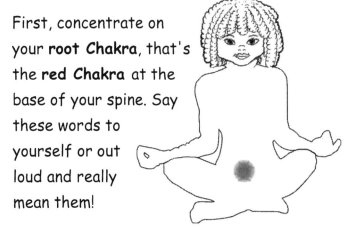

'I am grounded. I am safe and secure. The

Universe sends me all I need. The earth supports me. I am strong. I am confident. I am responsible for my own life. I trust in myself and I trust in the Universe. All is well.'

Now concentrate on your **2nd Chakra**, that's the **orange Chakra** above your red Chakra and just below your belly button. Say these words to yourself or out loud, and really mean them!

'I am creative. I do what I love doing. I share my gifts and my talents with others and I receive an abundance of gifts in return. I feel good about who I am. I love being me. I appreciate and am grateful for everything that I have.'

Chakras, Crystals, Colours and Drew the Dragon!

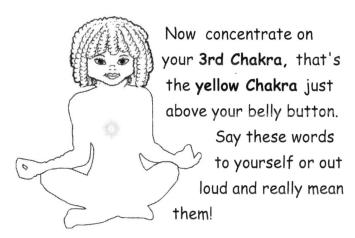

Now concentrate on your **3rd Chakra,** that's the **yellow Chakra** just above your belly button. Say these words to yourself or out loud and really mean them!

'I am confident in everything I do. I am full of energy and strength. I know I can make my dreams come true. I have the power to make people happy. I know I can be the best I can be.'

Now concentrate on your 4th Chakra, that's your **Heart Chakra, green** with little **speckles of pink,** where your heart is of course. Say these words either to yourself or out loud and really mean them!

'I am full of love for myself, for everybody else and for all forms of life. I am love. I love myself as I am, and I love and accept everybody else as they are. I do not judge or criticise myself or other people. I always follow my heart, because my heart guides me to do what is right.'

Now concentrate on your **5th Chakra,** that's your **Throat Chakra**, the **pale blue Chakra**. Say these words either to yourself or out loud and really mean them!

'I always speak the truth. I am careful what I say because I do not want to hurt anyone with my words. I express myself openly and honestly with my voice.'

Chakras, Crystals, Colours and Drew the Dragon!

Now concentrate on your **6th Chakra**, that's your **Third Eye Chakra,** right in the middle of your forehead, the **indigo Chakra**. Say these words either to yourself or out loud and really mean them!

'I sense things through my Third Eye that I cannot see with my other two eyes. I am intuitive. I can imagine great things. I get messages from God and the Angels through my Third Eye. I am calm. I see that I am perfect as I am right now. I see that I have nothing to prove either to myself or to anyone else. I see and understand that there is no such thing as making a mistake. Everything is a learning experience and I am ready to learn from everything that happens to me.'

Finally, now concentrate on your **7th Chakra**, your **Crown Chakra**, right at the top of your head, your **violet** or **purple Chakra**. Say these words either to yourself or out loud, and really mean them!

'I am connected to everything in the whole of Creation. I am connected to all other people, to all the animals, all the plants, and to God. This connection keeps me in balance with the entire universe. I feel very much at peace with myself and with everything in my life because I know I am connected to the great God Energy. Everything good is coming to me.'

You have just done a beautiful meditation exercise concentrating on your **7 Chakras** and their colours.

Here are some other affirmations you can say,

48

either to yourself or out loud. Affirmations are positive statements, and they make us feel good!

I am Love

I am loved

I love myself

I am Light

I am Divine

I am healthy

I am kindness

I am caring

I am wisdom

I am compassion

I am creative

I am sharing

I am perfection

Eileen McCourt

I am confident

I am forgiving

I am strong

I am energy

I am power

I am worthy

I am peace

I am free

I am happy

I am beautiful

I am safe

I am thankful

I am smart

I am listened to

I am good at making friends

Chakras, Crystals, Colours and Drew the Dragon!

WOW!

What an amazing, wonderful person *I AM !!!*

Can you think of any other words to describe how amazing and wonderful you really and truly are?

PART TWO: CRYSTALS

UNDERSTANDING CRYSTALS

Crystals, gems and stones, especially tumbled stones, are all very beautiful and appealing. They come from deep down inside the Earth, and so they are all a form of life. And because they are a form of life, they send out energy. Remember learning this in '**Rainbows, Angels and Unicorns**', where I explained all about energy and how we are all energy?

Did you know that the energy in crystals is so strong that there is a crystal in your watch, giving it the power it needs to keep ticking, and also in your computer and television? That's right! Crystals provide power and energy!

And since the beginning of time, they have been doing just that! They have been providing for early man what we now call electricity! The lost city of Atlantis had an enormous crystal

Chakras, Crystals, Colours and Drew the Dragon!

which gave the people all the power they needed. The ancient Egyptians used crystals, as did the Mayans and the Aztecs, and of course, the Native American Indians.

Every living thing has a consciousness. That means it has a certain level of understanding and vibrates at a particular rate. Crystals, gems and stones are all classed as solid matter, all vibrating at different rates, depending on the material out of which each is made.

Ancient civilizations believed that crystals had healing powers, and they used them to heal people, animals and plants. They believed that crystals held information about all sorts of things, information that could be retrieved and used. Just like the hard drive on your computer! It stores all sorts of information.

The hard drive on your computer has been programmed to store all that material. Crystals too, can be programmed to perform certain tasks. For example, when you buy a new crystal,

53

you can programme it to bring peace and calm to everyone who comes into your house. You don't always need to programme your crystals though, as they all know what particular task they have to do anyway! For example, rose quartz knows its job is to promote harmony and love.

And when you are choosing a crystal, it is not exactly you who is doing the choosing! It is actually the crystal that chooses you! It's all about energy again! The energy of the crystal likes your energy and decides it wants to be with you, and so it sends out energy vibes that attract you to it! How clever is that!

That's why you cannot really choose a crystal for anyone else! That person's energy is not your energy and the crystal might not like their energy! And you cannot give anyone a crystal that has been with you for a while, because the crystal is used to your energy now, and it will cause all sorts of problems if you give it away to someone else! It will upset the energy in their house, maybe make people argue and quarrel more than they usually do!

So you see, you have to treat your crystals with great respect. They are not just attractive decorations sitting around the place!

And they need to be cleansed and re-charged! Simply because they absorb the energies around them. And how do you cleanse and re-charge them?

All you have to do is set them outside in the moon-light. If you do not have a safe place to leave them outside overnight, then you can place them on a windowsill inside where they can absorb the moon's energy.

Yes, direct sunlight is good for them too, but only in short amounts, as the sunlight can fade them, whereas the light of the moon does not fade them.

Or you can cleanse them the way you cleanse your Chakras! Simply hold them in your hands, and imagine the great white light flowing over them, cleaning and clearing them.

You can place your tumbled stones under running water and imagine any negative energy being rinsed off them by the water. But not your crystals! Many crystals will dissolve in water! So be careful!

Chakras, Crystals, Colours and Drew the Dragon!

You can enjoy your beautiful crystals in many different ways. You can wear them as jewelry in bracelets or necklaces, or in your pocket, purse or handbag. You can keep them close to you when you feel you need their energy or protection, or under your pillow while you are sleeping.

If you love your crystals and treat them with respect, they will love you in return! How good is that!

Choosing your crystals

Chakras, Crystals, Colours and Drew the Dragon!

CRYSTAL COLOURS AND YOUR CHAKRAS

Crystals come in all sizes, shapes and colours.

And there is a colour of crystal to match each of your **7 Chakras!**

For your root Chakra, your **Red Chakra**: red jasper; red garnet; ruby; hematite; tourmaline.

For your **Orange Chakra**: orange calcite; carnelian.

For your **Yellow Chakra**:   yellow topaz; citrine; labradorite.

For your **Green / pink Chakra**: green calcite; rose quartz; tiger eye; aventurine; emerald; jade; malachite.

For your **Light blue Chakra**: turquoise; blue topaz; soddite; blue calcite; aquamarine; blue lace agate.

For your **Indigo / dark blue Chakra**: fluorite;

lapis lazuli; sodalite.

For your **Violet / purple Chakra**: Amethyst; clear quartz; angelite; selenite.

Let us look now at how you can clean and clear your chakras with these crystals!

CLEANSING YOUR CHAKRAS WITH CRYSTALS

Yes! You can use crystals to help you clean and clear your **7 Chakras**!

Remember, you can **programme** your crystals! All you have to do is mentally tell them what you want them to do for you!

In this exercise, you want your crystals to help you clear and clean your **7 Chakras**!

Maybe you already have a crystal to match the colour of each Chakra?

If not, then maybe your mum, dad, guardian or whoever is looking after you might take you to a crystal shop and let you choose for yourself a small crystal for each Chakra. Or maybe your birthday or Christmas is coming up! Most crystal shops and Angel shops sell a set of Chakra crystals in one box, or little tumble stones, one red, one orange, one yellow, one green, one blue, one indigo and one violet, one for each Chakra. And they are not expensive!

So let's see how we use these coloured crystals to clean our **7 Chakras**!

First, as always, find a quiet comfortable place to sit or lie down. Breathe deeply, breathing in the white light, and feel your entire body relax.

Now, take one of the **red crystals** in your hands, such as **red** jasper, **red** garnet, or ruby, or any of the other **red** crystals

Chakras, Crystals, Colours and Drew the Dragon!

associated with your **red root Chakra.** As you continue to hold the **red crystal**, place your hands over your root Chakra, your 1st Chakra, **your red Chakra**, and imagine the crystal pouring its colour into your **red Chakra**, filling it with beautiful **red light**, clearing and cleaning it, making it sparkle and glow. Stay for a few minutes, soaking in this beautiful **red light** from your crystal or tumble stone into your **red Chakra**.

Now change the red crystal in your hands for an **orange crystal** or tumble stone, to match **your orange Chakra**, your second Chakra. Choose from any of the crystals associated with this

creative Chakra, such as **orange** calcite or carnelian. Now, holding the crystal, place your hands over your **orange Chakra** and imagine the crystal pouring its **orange light** into your **orange Chakra**, filling it with its beautiful **orange light,** clearing and cleaning it, making it sparkle and glow. Stay for a few minutes, soaking in this beautiful **orange light** from your crystal or tumble stone into **your orange Chakra.**

Next, change the orange crystal for a **yellow crystal** or tumble stone, to match your 3rd Chakra, **your yellow**

Chakras, Crystals, Colours and Drew the Dragon!

Chakra. Choose from **yellow** topaz, citrine or any other crystal associated with your **yellow Chakra**. Do the same with this crystal as you did with the other two crystals, and feel the beautiful **yellow colour** pouring into your **yellow Chakra** from your **yellow crystal**, clearing and cleaning it, and making it sparkle and glow. Stay for a few minutes, allowing yourself to soak up this beautiful **yellow crystal energy** into your **yellow Chakra.**

Now for your 4th Chakra, your Heart Chakra, **green and pink**. Choose from one of the crystals or tumble stones associated with your Heart Chakra and do the same with it as you did with the others. You can choose from **green**

65

calcite, rose quartz, jade, emerald, or any of the others you read about in the previous chapter. Imagine your beautiful Heart Chakra being filled with this amazing energy from your crystal! Stay for a few minutes, enjoying this amazing feeling! Your Heart Chakra is being cleared and cleaned by the energy of your **green or pink crystal**!

Next, change your crystal for one associated with your **pale blue Throat Chakra**, your 5th Chakra. This time choose from the **blue range**, such as **blue** topaz, **blue** calcite,

Chakras, Crystals, Colours and Drew the Dragon!

aquamarine or **blue** lace agate. Now holding your crystal, place your hands above your Throat Chakra and feel the beautiful **blue colour** pouring from your **blue crystal** into your **blue Throat Chakra**, clearing and cleaning it. Stay for a few minutes, allowing yourself to soak up all this beautiful energy into your **blue Throat Chakra**.

Change your crystal again, this time for one associated with your 6th Chakra, **your indigo Third Eye Chakra**. Choose from lapis lazuli, sodalite, or

fluorite, for example. Now place your crystal on your

67

Third Eye and feel the energy from your crystal pouring into your Third Eye, clearing and cleaning it. Stay a few minutes allowing your Third Eye to soak up this beautiful energy from this beautiful crystal.

Finally, your 7th Chakra, **your violet or purple Crown Chakra**. Choose the **purple** amethyst, or clear quartz, two of the most powerful of all the crystals! Hold it in your hands above your Crown Chakra and sense the colour from your amazing crystal pouring

into your 7th Chakra, clearing and cleaning it. Stay for a few minutes, allowing your Crown Chakra to soak up this amazing energy from your beautiful crystal.

Thank all your crystals for working for you in such a wonderful way!

Eileen McCourt

ENERGY OF COLOURS

You know now all the different colours of your **7 Chakras**!

And the different colours of crystals and tumble stones!

Yes, colour is very important in our lives!

Imagine how boring and drab life would be if there no colours!

Thankfully, colour is all around us, everywhere! The colours in Nature, in the trees and flowers, the sky, the ocean, the mountains and rocks, the autumn leaves! All so beautiful!

Remember reading in **'Rainbows, Angels and Unicorns'** how everything is energy and all energy vibrates at a certain frequency?

Well, colours are all energy too! And they all vibrate at different frequencies! That means that every colour has a different effect on us when we see it!

And the colour of whatever it is we are looking at can make us like or dislike it!

For example, many people do not like spiders! Have you ever wondered why? A fear of spiders is called arachnophobia. Have you ever wondered why so many people have a reaction to spiders? Could it be because of the colour of them?

Now if you colour that spider in with your favourite colour, does it look different? More attractive? More likeable? Try it and see! Could you even now perhaps like it as a pet?

Lady birds are little bugs too, but they appeal to people much more than most bugs! Could that be because they are coloured red, making them more attractive and pretty?

Chakras, Crystals, Colours and Drew the Dragon!

All the colours of the flowers too! Have you ever wondered why they are all different? Could it be because they are meant to attract bees and birds? If they were all just black or white, would that have the same effect?

Yes! Colour plays a very important part in our lives!

When the traffic lights go red, we stop. When they turn to orange, we get ready to go again. And when they turn green, we are on our way!

Think about how colours make you feel!

For example, when you are in the dentist's or doctor's waiting room.

Have you noticed how the walls are painted?

Chakras, Crystals, Colours and Drew the Dragon!

They are usually a pale blue or green. That's because pale blue and green are what we call relaxing, calming colours. All meant to calm you down!

How about the walls of your classroom? What colours are they? Black? Brown? Or are they all bright colours? Probably! And why? To give you energy of course! To brighten you up!

The same with children's playgrounds! All bright colours! To cheer everyone up!

Chakras, Crystals, Colours and Drew the Dragon!

And the walls of your bedroom? What colours are they? Black? I don't think so! You would be sooooooooo depressed!

Or your baby sister's or baby brother's clothes? Or their cot? All black or dark colours? Most definitely not!

And how does your mummy get you to eat food that is good for you? By putting lots of colour on your plate of course!

If everything were black or dark colours, would you want to eat it?

If sweets were all dark colours, would you buy them?

If ice-cream was black? **YUCK!**

Colour in your favourite ice cream and sprinkles!

Think of uniforms! In hospitals, white is often worn, and the walls are usually white as well. That is to make you feel that the place is very clean and sterile. That means there are no germs hanging around!

Chakras, Crystals, Colours and Drew the Dragon!

White is also a summer colour. You probably wear lots of white in the summer, but not in winter.

Business men and women, security guards, police men and police women all usually wear dark clothes, which gives the impression that they are very serious about their job and very reliable.

Now, can you think what these colours might suggest to people?

Chakras, Crystals, Colours and Drew the Dragon!

Green?

Pink?

Red?

Yellow?

Brown?

Black?

Turquoise?

Blue?

Think too about the colour of your parents' car!

The colour of the clothes you wear?

The colour of the clothes your mum wears?

The colour of the clothes your dad wears? Your brothers and sisters?

What does this all tell you about them?

We often associate colours with feelings too!

For example, we say:

'I'm in the red'

'I'm in the pink'

'I'm in the black'

'Green with envy'

'Green fingers'

'Green pastures'

'Greenhorn!'

'Blue with cold'

'Feeling blue'

'Shrinking violet'

'A gray area', meaning not very clear

'Red with anger'

'Red-hot''

Red light'

Chakras, Crystals, Colours and Drew the Dragon!

'A red rag to a bull'

'White with fear'

'He's yellow!' meaning he is a coward

'The white flag', meaning you are surrendering.

'Green card'

'Yellow card'

'Red card'

'You're a real peach!'

Can you think of any other expressions we use that are associated with colours?

How about 'I'm browned off'? We all say that from time to time!

How many more can you think of?

Finally, did you know that you can sense colours? That you can sense them through the energy vibration each gives off?

Try this experiment!

Cut up strips of paper all of different colours. Place them all in front of you on the table. Now close your eyes tightly. No peeping! Let your hand pass over the different colours and see if you can sense which colour is which. You might just surprise yourself!

Chakras, Crystals, Colours and Drew the Dragon!

THE 7 COLOURS OF THE RAINBOW

How beautiful is a rainbow! WOW!

Most people notice when there is a rainbow in the sky. How could they not?

BUT! While most people **SEE** the rainbow, very few of them actually know how to **EXPERIENCE** the rainbow!

So how do you *experience*, and not just notice or *see* the rainbow?

Well, it's very simple, now that you know all about your **7 Chakras**!

Yes, **7 Chakras**! And how many colours in the rainbow?

Yes! **7 colours** in the rainbow!

And guess what? They are all the same! Is that not amazing?

Is that not just amazing that the same **7 colours of your 7 Chakras** are the same **7 colours** that are in the rainbow?

Red

Orange

Yellow

Green

Blue

Indigo

Violet

Your body is a rainbow!

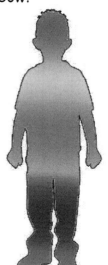

Chakras, Crystals, Colours and Drew the Dragon!

Remember!

You have just learned in the previous chapter how every colour is a vibration, sending out energy.

Well, next time when you see a rainbow in the sky, think of this!

The colour **red** in the rainbow is attracted to the **red** in your **red root Chakra**! So it is beaming down energy into your **red Chakra**!

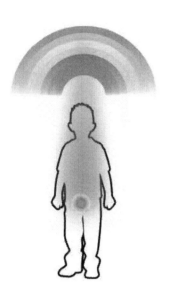

The colour **orange** in the rainbow is attracted to the **orange** in your **orange Chakra**! So it is beaming down energy into your **orange Chakra**!

The colour **yellow** in the rainbow is attracted to the **yellow** in your **yellow Chakra**! So it is beaming down energy into your **yellow Chakra**!

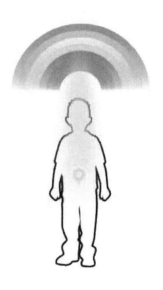

Chakras, Crystals, Colours and Drew the Dragon!

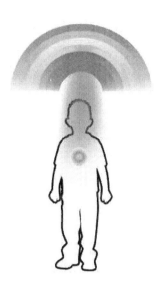

The colour **green** in the rainbow is attracted to the **green** in your **green Heart Chakra**! So it is beaming down energy into your **green Chakra**!

The colour **blue** in the rainbow is attracted to the **blue** in your **blue Throat Chakra**! So it is beaming down energy into your **blue Throat Chakra**!

The colour **indigo** in the rainbow is attracted to the **indigo** in your **Third Eye Chakra**! So it is beaming down energy into your **indigo Third Eye**!

The colour **violet** in the rainbow is attracted to the **violet** in your **violet Crown Chakra**! So it is beaming down energy into your **violet Crown Chakra**!

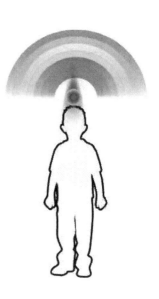

Chakras, Crystals, Colours and Drew the Dragon!

See what has just happened between **you and the rainbow**?

You have just had a super charge of energy from the rainbow filling up your **7 Chakras**!

WOW!

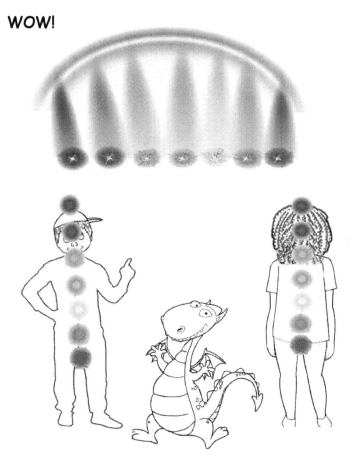

Eileen McCourt

HAVING A RAINBOW SHOWER

Now here is an exercise that you will just love!

Having a rainbow shower!

Again, all you need is your imagination!

As always, find a quiet and comfortable place to sit or lie down.

Close your eyes. Breathe deeply.

Chakras, Crystals, Colours and Drew the Dragon!

Imagine you are in the shower. See the water coming flowing down over your body, and feel it washing away all your worries and concerns and anything that may be annoying you or bothering you.

Watch as the murky water becomes clearer as it washes everything away from you that you do not want.

Now see the water as crystal clear. Everything that you do not want has been washed away! Gone for good!

Now imagine the rainbow sending a shower down over you in all the different colours. Feel the energy of all the colours flowing down over you, filling your entire body with peace and calm and strength.

Stay there for as long as you wish, just enjoying the wonderful feeling of all the colours flowing down over you.

When you are ready, imagine the rainbow turning off. Slowly open your eyes.

Now, how do you feel?

Amazing, no doubt!

Did you know that you can also buy a colour shower head for your shower, that can be very easily attached to your shower, causing the water to come out and down over you in all the

Chakras, Crystals, Colours and Drew the Dragon!

different colours?

How cool is that!

Perhaps you could ask your mum or dad to buy one on the internet for you?

Wouldn't that be just awesome?

Eileen McCourt

Chakras, Crystals, Colours and Drew the Dragon!

Eileen McCourt

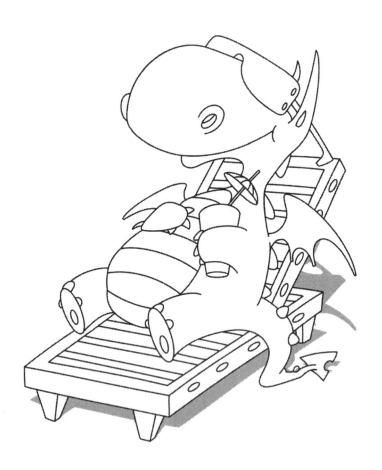

Chakras, Crystals, Colours and Drew the Dragon!

Eileen McCourt

How did you do? Did you get my colours right? Have you coloured me in correctly?

Chakras, Crystals, Colours and Drew the Dragon!

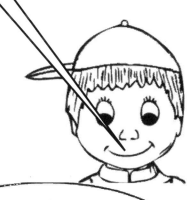

Sadly it's time for us to go now! Until we meet again, remember you need to keep your 7 chakras cleansed, sparkling and balanced! And don't forget to brighten up your life with bright colours and beautiful crystals!

We've enjoyed meeting you again and we've had great fun learning all about Chakras, crystals and colours. We hope you have had fun too!

Eileen McCourt

BYE!

Chakras, Crystals, Colours and Drew the Dragon!

Here is copy of the front cover of this book for you to colour in. Let your imagination run wild!

Eileen McCourt

If you would like some more pictures of Drew the dragon to colour in, you can download them by visiting my webpage:

http://bit.ly/2JM8Qfy

Chakras, Crystals, Colours and Drew the Dragon!

Other children's books by Eileen McCourt

Rainbows, Angels and Unicorns!

Ideal for younger Children

Eileen McCourt

Life's But A Game

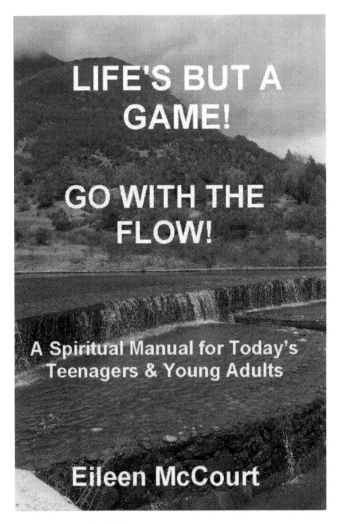

Ideal for young Teenagers

Printed in Great Britain
by Amazon